Called to Serve as a School Governor

Alison Farnell

Consultant in Christian Education

GROVE BOOKS LIMITED

RIDLEY HALL RD CAMBRIDGE CB3 9HU

Contents

Acknowledgment

As a governor I have worked alongside many people who have inspired me and shaped both my thinking and my governance practice. Many of them appear in this book. Some, but not all of these colleagues, share my Christian faith. This book represents what I believe and what I hope I practise, based on, or refined by, the example and practice of those with whom I have worked.

Whilst working together for CARE for Education in the 1990s, Carol Dadswell, Ann Holt, Mike Simmonds and I published numerous resources about being a Christian governor. I am hugely indebted to them and they will recognize some of the fruits of our collaborative thinking in this book! They have been invaluable friends and fellow travellers on my journey as a governor.

I would also like to thank Judy Burgess, Richard Cooke, Trevor Cooling, Ruth Eade, Richard Farnell, Rob Fox, Peter French, Michael Langrish, Mary McKay, Anthony McLaren, John Murray, Sally Smith, Eric Wood and the head teachers, members of staff and governing bodies at the schools where I have served. In different ways, they have each helped to write this book.

Disclaimer

All the examples of school governing in this book are based on actual instances. Names have been changed to protect and respect anonymity.

First Impression October 2010

ISSN 2041-0964

ISBN 978 1 85174 773 3

1 Introduction

I believe that God *calls* Christians to be school governors. But, like most Christian governors, when I started on my governing journey I do not think I recognized that I was called to serve in this way, nor did I understand what it meant.

You could say that I became a school governor because one of our daughters died. When our toddler son was joined by healthy, almost full-term twin sisters, we had our hands full and felt very blessed by God! Life was joyous, busy, exhausting and fun. When, at three months old, one of our daughters died suddenly, apparently as a cot death, our lives went on hold, freeze-framed by shock, grief and big, big questions. It was several months later that our vicar asked, 'Would you help me? We have a vacancy for a foundation governor, and I thought of you. Would you consider it?' His wise invitation helped me re-engage with life beyond our family and I became a school governor.

Throughout this booklet, the reader will be able to consider whether, how and why God calls Christians to serve as school governors in any and all types of schools. I have included examples of Christian governors serving in both community schools and church schools and these two situations are, no doubt, different. By including actual examples, I hope to enable the reader to consider the impact that being an effective Christian governor can make in whichever school God has put you. I believe it is about joining in with what God is already doing in his world and contributes to establishing God's kingdom here and now. One reader of the draft manuscript commented, 'It showed me what it means to *be* a Christian school governor, not just what to *do*.'

Being an effective Christian governor contributes to establishing God's kingdom

2 School Governing: What Are You Letting Yourself in For?

The Education System

In 1979, state schools in England had governors who met with the head teacher each term; they lunched or took tea together and chatted amiably about the school. A seismic shift happened in 1986; since then, change has been constant with regular Education Acts, fresh jargon and soon-to-be-forgotten acronyms. Similar changes took place in the rest of the UK, to governing bodies in Wales and to school boards in Northern Ireland, while school boards in Scotland morphed into parents' councils.

In 1979, it was established that 99% of UK children will spend eleven years, or over 15,000 hours, minimum in school by the time they reach the end of secondary education. So schooling matters! Whilst parenting and home life are the foremost influence on a child's development, school experience has a massive effect on a child's life chances. Any doubts about this were dispelled by the Children's Society Report (2009), *A Good Childhood: Searching for Values in a Competitive Age*. Ensuring that schools offer the best education possible is the combined responsibility of a range of individuals and agencies including school governors. Since every school has a governance structure of some sort, school governors are the largest group of volunteers nationally, currently around 350,000.[1] Governors have considerable responsibility and can significantly influence a school for good (or ill). In England, governing bodies are now subject to rigorous OFSTED inspection, and Church of England schools also undergo Statutory Inspection of Anglican Schools (SIAS).

Governors are the largest group of volunteers nationally

Historically, the church played an extremely important role in establishing schooling in the UK. In most cases, early public schooling was provided by church initiatives.[2] As a consequence of the 1944 Education Act, church schools were established as either Voluntary Aided (VA) schools or Voluntary Controlled (VC) schools. The Roman Catholic Church retained all its schools as VA in 1944, whereas the Church of England schools became a mixture of VA and VC schools. In a VA school, the church foundation has a majority on the governing body, employs the staff and is responsible for some capital costs. In a VC school, the church foundation is in the minority on the governing body and the Local Authority remains as the employer. Today, church schools, with the large majority being primary schools, account for between a quarter and a third of the total number of schools in England.

Church schools have variously been labelled 'denominational schools,' 'schools with a religious character' or 'faith schools.' Immediately prior to the 2010 General Election, the National College of School Leadership reverted to the term 'schools with a religious character,' which seems the most appropriate definition. Whilst today Christian schools still constitute the large majority of such schools, there are now also Jewish, Hindu, Sikh and Muslim schools under the same umbrella.

Within the state sector there is a huge variety of type of schools. Beyond the state sector, there are independent schools, many with Christian foundations, and what are known as New Christian Schools (usually established by groups of Christian parents or churches). A substantial number of families choose to homeschool their children, some due to Christian convictions about education. With the exception of homeschooling, every school has a governance structure of some sort, to which the fundamental principles of governing apply.

Governing Schools

Governors are 'part of the strategic leadership of the school, helping to set its direction and leading it into the future, which is likely to be one of constant change.'[3] Currently, improving educational standards, promoting community cohesion and efficiency of operation are key issues. Whatever the particular focus of the moment, a school governing body's work, undertaken in partnership with the professional staff employed to work in or with the school, is about a strategic role related to promoting high standards of education and achievement.

With the Headteacher, School Governors Set the Strategic Direction

They develop a vision for the school, with aims and objectives, then plan targets and policies and make decisions to bring that about.

> As the vicar, James ensured that he was joined on the governing body of the parish VC school by two other effective foundation governors. He also offered to be a community governor in a community school in the parish. His involvement was welcomed and he worked with the head teacher on a consultation exercise to re-examine the vision, values and aims of the school. The outcome was a strategic direction for the community school which was totally compatible with Christian belief. In the process, all governors discussed the Christian beliefs underpinning the shared values to which all the stakeholders subscribed.

School Governors Act as Critical Friends

This entails building solid, respectful and trustworthy relationships between governors and the staff team, so that governors can ask challenging questions of the head teacher and school leadership team.

> Carol, as chair of governors, met fortnightly with the head for an open conversation about anything which either of them needed to discuss. A relationship of respect, confidence and trust developed. Consequently, difficult and contentious issues, where governors rightly needed to question, explore or challenge decisions made by the head, could be aired in a supportive environment, prior to taking the discussion to the full governors' meeting. It also gave the head a suitable context to register to the chair of governors the head's disquiet about certain actions and behaviour of some governors!

School Governors Ensure Accountability

Working with all the available information, governors monitor the progress of the implementation of the strategy, evaluate the outcomes and give account to parents, the community and government.

> With the introduction of a new national teachers' salary structure, a new staffing structure was needed at the school where Jane was a governor. Redundancies were inevitable. A committee of governors was thoroughly involved with the head teacher at all stages. This gave the necessary accountability by ensuring that the correct procedures were followed and that outcomes were just.

Research into what makes a successful school points consistently to the importance of the school leadership. Arguably, therefore, the most significant job governors do is appointing the head teacher. The beliefs of the head will profoundly shape the future direction of the school. In a church VA school, it is possible to advertise for a Christian head as this is described as a Genuine Occupational Requirement (GOR). This is not the case in a church VC school. However, it is possible for VC school governors to define responsibilities for church school distinctives in a job description and particular characteristics in a person specification.

> Having been a governor in several different schools, Anji has been involved in the appointment of six head teachers, three acting head and eight deputy heads. Looking back, she can track the changes that happened in each school as a consequence of these appointments.

The make-up of each governing body varies depending on the school's constitution or instrument of governance; in England these were all revised for 1 September 2006. Individual governors may be elected, chosen, invited or even be there by default, as the role came with their job (this is true of some head teachers; clergy may be *ex officio* governors of a parish school). Each usually has a fixed term of appointment. The governing body has corporate responsibility for decisions that must yield the best outcome for the education of the pupils in the school. Individual governors (apart from the chairman in certain circumstances) cannot act alone.

School governance in England is a stakeholder model; each governor usually represents a particular constituency. Yet they are not delegates who can be mandated to speak or vote in a particular way. Governors may represent parents, school staff, the Local Authority, the community, the foundation church or organization (in VA and VC schools) or even the sponsors or partners in academies and trust schools. Christians become governors in all types of school and in each of these categories.

Inevitably all governors, acting with integrity and authenticity, will bring their own beliefs and values into their governing role. No-one is neutral. Humanist, Hindu, Muslim and secular colleagues will each have their own perspective on an issue. Similarly, Christians' beliefs will shape their contributions; they must learn to express this in ways which are relevant to other governors. Ultimately, as in all ethical decision-making, the outcome of a discussion in a governing body might need to be a negotiated way forward.

> Mike, a foundation governor, chaired the governors' appointment panel for the new head at the church VC school, situated in an area with a high percentage of pupils from ethnic minorities. Given that foundation governors form a minority on a VC governing body, the panel had to negotiate agreement about the person specification and job description. Eventually they agreed to precede the detail of the person specification with the wording, 'The governors hope to appoint a Christian who…' In the job description, they clearly set out that the person appointed would be responsible for strengthening the church school ethos and the spiritual development of the pupils. The process was supported by prayer in the parish church. An excellent Sikh head teacher was appointed. Because he recognized the importance of faith in his own life and in that of others, he ensured that connections with the parish church were deepened, that Christian volunteers were involved in many aspects of the school life, that the church members led collective worship every week and that spirituality was recognized as part of pupils' entitlement in the curriculum.

Church School or Community School?

Whether Christian governors play a more important role in community schools or church schools is an interesting missiological question. In church schools, governors are working in a context where the Christian faith is regarded as the norm, not the exception. This provides particular responsibilities and opportunities for the church's mission. Christian governors in a community school usually need to earn respect and credibility with other governor colleagues before any specifically Christian views they express can be heard, understood and accepted.

Governing in a Church School

Lord Dearing, in *The Way Ahead: Church of England Schools in the New Millennium,* introduced a clear challenge that church schools 'must be distinctively Christian' and 'places where the Christian faith is alive and practised.'[4] Whilst recognizing that this distinctiveness is something which has to be worked out appropriately by each governing body in the context within which their school is located, Dearing suggested that, as a minimum, it might include:

- appointing a head teacher committed to establishing and maintaining the school's Christian character
- daily, meaningful Christian worship
- incorporating Christian values into school life
- ensuring high quality RE
- observing major Christian festivals, and ensuring that pupils from faiths other than Christianity are able to mark their festivals with integrity
- active relationship with the parish church
- using appropriate Christian signs and symbols

Given that the vast majority of church schools serve diverse communities, comprising all faiths and none, church schools have been recognized recently for their excellent contribution to community cohesion.[5] The 'Christian distinctiveness' concept describing church schools in *The Way Ahead* has subsequently evolved into describing church schools as 'distinctive and inclusive.'

The Archbishop of Canterbury, the Rowan Williams, developed this theme in relation to Church of England academies (and other types of school) in an address in October 2009.[6] He explained his belief that the church's role in education is about giving people the tools they need for living, and he chose justice and liberation as the hallmarks of Christian distinctiveness. This provides a particularly appropriate rationale for the church's investment in areas of severe social deprivation through founding academies and other schools.

In the first book in this series, *Church Schools: a Mission-shaped Vision,* Tim Elbourne develops some interesting models of mission relating to church schools and understanding their role in the life of the church today. Church school governors will benefit from reflecting on exactly how their church school and the church are involved together as co-workers in the activity of God in the world. Tim suggests that 'its schools are part of what the Church of England *is* and not simply one of the projects or activities the church *does*.'

Governing as a Christian Ministry

Fifteen years into my career as a governor, another vicar of our church wisely challenged me. I was then teaching part time and was chair of governors at a local Church of England secondary school. My husband was involved in a demanding job, with various other commitments, and we had three school-age children. I was responsible for the Sunday morning children's activities at church and I was struggling to keep all the balls in the air. Our vicar challenged me to decide which was my main area of ministry and to let the others go. The model of ministry of a three-legged stool, with skills, gifts and passion as the three legs, helped me to recognize that my main ministry was in school governing. The vicar supported my decision to give up the Sunday morning children's work. He recognized, blessed and released me into ministry in school governance. At last I had recognized that, at least for the moment, I was called to serve as a school governor.

3 Why Would You Become a School Governor?

It is a Good Thing to Do

School governing can be an immensely fulfilling voluntary role. It brings huge responsibility and, depending on the school's context and the current situation, it can also be tough and at times generate stress and tension. Governing bodies need people who understand what is meant by confidentiality, and they usually adopt the Nolan principles of public life—selflessness, integrity, objectivity, accountability, openness, honesty and leadership. Governors need to have time to give to the role, occasionally be free to visit while pupils are in school, have a reasonable degree of literacy and be able to contribute to discussion in a constructive manner. They also have to be comfortable working with committees! Some may have particular expertise to offer to the governing body, but the governors' guru, Joan Sallis, is often quoted as saying that 'the precious light of ordinariness must be allowed to shine on expert activities, if these activities are to remain healthy.'

When I first became a governor it seemed a good thing to do at the time. Yes, I prayed about the decision, but I did not have a profound sense of God *calling me* into this ministry. All the Christian governors introduced through this booklet became governors in different ways. Yet they have all found that they not only had something to contribute but also gained enormously from their involvement. So why did they get involved?

- *The community governor:* Judith decided to use her considerable financial background as a community governor. God had given her opportunity, experience and expertise and she wanted to put something back into her local community.
- *The parent governor:* Linda had some time to spare as her children began school. Being a multi-tasking mum, she was gifted at managing situations, conflict resolution, balancing budgets, sorting out problems and asking challenging questions. She was unsure what she had to offer as a governor, but was persuaded by friends at church to stand for election as a parent governor in their children's school, and brought that 'precious light of ordinariness' onto the governing body.

- *The Local Authority governor:* Mike was an accounts manager who lived, dreamed and breathed spreadsheets, targets and budgets. The school which his children would eventually attend needed to recruit a Local Authority governor as none of the local councillors wanted to take it on. Another parent at Mike's church, who was already a governor, recognized that his expertise would be really useful to support the governors.
- *The staff governor:* Dave was not sure where God was leading him in his teaching career. He stood for election as the staff governor because no one else would do it and he thought it would look good on his CV! Looking back, he realized that it had been invaluable preparation for his promotion into school leadership.
- *The foundation governor:* Andrew retired from senior leadership in a secondary school where he was known for the integrity of his Christian faith at work. Not wanting to lose contact with schools and pupils, and believing that he could still give something of benefit to a school, he offered to fill the gap as a foundation governor at one of the feeder primary schools.
- *The vicar (ex officio governor)*: Arriving in her first parish as the vicar, looking forward to learning the ropes as she had never having been a governor before, Sue took up her *ex officio* governor at the church VC school. Within three months she was asked to become chairperson, as it was recognized that she was the only person with sufficient skill to manage and reconcile the squabbling factions in the governing body.

When these Christians became school governors did they sense God calling them to serve in this way? Probably not. Like me, it was simply the right thing to do. School governing made good use of the gifts that God had given them: they each made very helpful contributions to the schools which they served. Following in the Celtic monastic tradition of integrated lifestyle, they chose godly discipline, pursuing their deepest convictions by serving others with their time, money and talents.

God Calls His People

'Being a school governor seems to be a good thing to do. I'm doing it because…' It took me many years of being a governor before I even thought about any sort of theological rationale for what I was doing, and I continue to learn and understand more about why, as a Christian, I am called to serve as a governor.

Understanding of Humankind

When I lead training sessions with church school staff and governors, we sometimes discuss questions such as 'What characterizes a good school?' and 'What characterizes a Christian school?' A stock answer to the second question is 'Christian values—like caring for every pupil.' It then only takes a moment to realize that most Christian values, like caring, are also values shared with colleagues of no particular faith, or who belong to faiths other than Christianity. So they are not distinctively Christian. However, one crucial distinctive is our Christian understanding of what makes us human.

Christians believe that people are made in the image of God. He breathed his Spirit into them, he loves them and went as far as to sacrifice his own son to redeem their sin. So, when governors and teachers are working on vision, aims or values statements for their school and want to include values like respect, care and love, and statements such as 'every child is special,' it is straightforward for Christian governors in a community school to agree to such shared values because they are compatible with Christian belief. However, in church schools these statements can also explicitly reflect the Christian understanding of what it means to be human. So it might read, 'Because each person is unique and loved by God, we will respect, love and care for all members of our school community.'

> Many governors are familiar with the idea of setting *SMART* targets (*S*trategic, *M*easurable, *A*chievable, *R*ealistic, *T*ime limited). Mike Simmonds, working for CARE for Education in 1997, suggested that Christian governors could encourage schools to introduce *GRACE* targets, *G*od *R*especting *A*nd *C*hild *E*nabling. Eric Wood, when he was Chief Education Officer in Warwickshire, suggested that schools should have at least one *SOUL* target, focusing on spirituality.

Metaphors Related to Establishing the Kingdom of God

Christian governors are usually quick to identify their impact in a school as being like 'salt and light' (Matthew 5.13) or 'leaven in the dough' (Matthew 13.33). Forensic scientists assume that 'every contact leaves a trace.' Finding the saltiness of a Christian governor should not be so difficult to detect, as salt flavours and preserves. In another sense, the Christian governor is 'the fragrance of Christ' (2 Corinthians 2.14–15), his presence in the school. Light brings hope, illumination, reassurance, understanding and wisdom, and Christian governors have the opportunity to bring the light of Christ into schools. As the leaven in the dough, Christian governors might need to speak out to redress the balance in what is a predominantly secular mindset in the world of education. This approach to Christian living has been described as a transformational model.

It is often assumed that Christian governors only care about sex education, RE and collective worship. Believing that Christians needed to be involved in all aspects of the school, Beth has variously been the governor responsible for literacy, numeracy and, currently, safeguarding.

If all of that seems quite challenging, we might well be encouraged by yet another metaphor that Jesus used (Matthew 17.20) and realize that even if we have faith as small as a mustard seed, it can have powerful effects!

There are some outstanding church schools which are true 'beacons on a hill' (Matthew 5.14–16). Where Christians are involved as governors in such schools, the gospel imperative is to let that light shine around. That could mean sharing the good practice with other schools so that they can improve things for their pupils also. In the competitive education culture of the 1990s and early 2000s, such collaboration and cooperation was counter-cultural. Although this is now encouraged by government, much more collaboration could benefit pupils' education.[7]

Chase C of E Primary School was judged to be outstanding in all respects. St John's C of E school, with complex educational challenges, had some excellent examples of good practice yet was judged to be barely satisfactory. These schools are near neighbours but separated by a major railway line. It takes just three minutes to drive between the schools, yet they are totally different socially and ethnically. When the Chase governors approved a plan proposed by the two heads for regular exchanges for collaborative working, they anticipated opposition from their pupils' parents so needed courage for their decision. Both schools gained from the collaboration, education was enriched in both schools and teachers learned from each other's good practice in teaching and learning. The light from the 'beacons' was allowed to shine more widely.

Speaking About Christian Faith

I suspect that St Francis of Assisi's exhortation to Christians to 'preach the gospel constantly, and if necessary, use words' is often used as an excuse never to admit to their Christian faith. Certainly the way Christians live is critical if they are to honour God. Yet they must not forget to 'be prepared to give an answer to everyone who asks you to give the reason for the hope that you have' (1 Peter 3.15). Peter continues, 'But do this with gentleness and respect.'

When Jesus sent out his disciples to take the good news of the kingdom (Luke 10), he sent them out in pairs. This seems to be an important biblical principle which churches might well consider when encouraging Christians to become school governors. Two or three Christian governors working together to support the school can usually achieve a great deal for the kingdom.

> In the community school where she was the chairperson, Chris actively encouraged Christians from a number of different churches, with suitable skills and gifts, to become involved as governors. Some stood for election as parent or staff governors, another joined as a Local Authority governor and another as a community governor. This meant that at any one time, there were usually at least two Christian governors on any committee or working group. Following Peter's injunction (above), they, with 'gentleness and respect' were able to bring their Christian voice into many discussions on the governing body.

Involvement in Community

By involvement in the education system as school governors Christians take an active part in God's redemptive work, caring for the world and humankind, helping to reconcile all of creation to God (Colossians 1.15–20). Christians are called to live a life which demonstrates that redeeming power of God. Where better to do that than in a school context?

Isaiah describes what God wants to see happen in communities where those who worship God are part of, and in partnership with, the wider community (Isaiah 65.20–23). Part of the Isaiah vision is that children are kept safe and do not die.[8]

For many Christians involved in school governing, they are indeed working out the Isaiah vision for children, seeking to provide excellent educational opportunities for holistic development. This might just mean ensuring provision for spiritual and moral development as required by the Education (Schools) Act 1992.[9] Conscious of the 'Every Child Matters' agenda and practising 'joined up thinking,' it might even mean ensuring that necessary welfare support is available. In some extreme cases, given the safeguarding issues in some schools, governors are actively involved in ensuring that children do not actually die, not just in the metaphorical, spiritual sense.

> The Every Child Matters (ECM) agenda has become part of educational vocabulary: schools should support children to be healthy, stay safe, enjoy and achieve, make a positive contribution and achieve economic well-being. In the initial discussion about ECM at the governing body, one governor suggested that spirituality was missing from the ECM agenda, and proposed that it be added as a sixth strand. Margaret was able to explain that she believed that, to make any difference in a pupil's life, it was essential for a spiritual dimension to underpin each of the five

ECM strands. As a result, the school's ECM policy was redrafted and the resulting work in school was based on this more holistic concept.

Many Christian governors are seeking to achieve Isaiah's vision by trying to bring about just and equitable solutions to today's education challenges and working to bring about *shalom* in our school communities. This may well mean speaking up for the poor and the oppressed, taking the side of those who have no voice to speak out for themselves and seeking justice.

For most schools in the state system, funding results from a complicated formula constructed by central government, which is then devolved to Local Authorities to distribute. In the mid 1990s, this formula took into account, and compensated for, a number of deprivation factors such as extreme rural problems and inner-city deprivation. Consequently, the allocation to a number of counties in the middle of England, where the socio-economic statistical measures just fell outside of the deprivation boundaries, meant that pupils in their schools were funded to a significantly lower level than pupils in immediately surrounding Education Authorities. Alison, as chair of the County Governors' Association, was part of a delegation of governors, councillors and Education Authority officials which lobbied Parliament to revise the central funding formula. Slightly more equitable funding resulted.

The principles of *shalom* are very evident in the current emphasis on developing community cohesion in schools. Recent research has demonstrated that in their community cohesion work, many church schools have a clear, shared vision and understanding of humankind and of the way that God intends us to live. [10]

Near to Matt's school is a site used by travellers, resented by the village community. Relationships between the two communities were often tense. The governors supported Matt in establishing a parents' forum to advise on aspects of the school's development. The representatives were handpicked by the staff to get a balanced representation of all types of parent. This gave the traveller parents representation on the parents' forum. Through working together, the parents discovered that, whether from the village or the travellers' site, they all cared deeply about their child's education. This was the beginning of better community relations throughout the whole area.

Seeking the Welfare of the City

Every school in England and Wales is in a parish—so potentially is linked to a church of some denomination. Yet recruiting governors for schools in the more deprived areas of our cities is a huge challenge. Vacancies can go unfilled for years. Christians from other parishes in the city have a real opportunity, even responsibility, to get involved in such schools as community, Local Authority and foundation governors.

There are plenty of examples from the early church of Christians getting involved in the leadership and governance of their cities, simply 'to seek the welfare of the city.'[11] Over a third of references to 'the church' in the New Testament are to a church in a city. The contribution those early Christians made to their cities was respected and accepted because of the integrity of their lives. This was faith in action for the good of the community and God worked through them to bring about his kingdom. Their significant contributions brought no reward other than the welfare of their city. It was seen as part of their discipleship and service. So the early church was a practical apologetic, showing a new way of life, embodying and incarnating the gospel of the kingdom. Today, many Christian school governors are doing exactly this.

In many deprived areas, whether inner-city or outer estates, some parents lack either the skills needed or the courage and self-confidence to believe that they have anything to offer as a governor. School might be a bad memory from their own past, preventing them from engaging as a governor. Language and cultural difficulties are frequently additional barriers in diverse ethnic communities, especially where migration creates a transient school population.

> There are currently 21 languages spoken by pupils in the Church of England school where John is a foundation governor. The community consists of recent arrivals from EU countries, an established Asian population and a number of white English families; many live on state benefits. None of the parents has any involvement with the parish church. The overall number of pupils in the school remains much the same throughout the year, but this masks the turnover in the community as families move in and out. Eventually, as a result of relationships built by one of the foundation governors regularly meeting and greeting parents in the playground, one parent had the courage to be co-opted as an associate governor.

Learning From Scripture

Governors, and schools as we know them, are not mentioned in the Bible. So how, as Christians, should we think theologically about involvement in education? 'What would Jesus do?' is a useful refrain, but governors usually need to know what Jesus would do *here* and *now*. Scripture does not always give us obvious answers to the issues we might need to address such as excluded pupils, allocation of resources and deficit budgets. But we can be guided by principles which are central to the whole of Scriptural revelation. If we explore the Bible with the governing issues we face in mind, we are likely to discover new God-given insights. Paul Marshall reminds us that we must 'shine the light of Scripture on all the questions that lie before us on our pilgrimage,' and to 'study the world in the light of the Word, and to know the world biblically.'[12]

Doing just that, a Christian governor, whether serving in a church school or a community school, can apply biblical beliefs and principles to discussion about the strategy and policy framework within which the school operates, and against which it will be judged and held to account. Principles such as the value of each individual, respect, neighbour-love, justice and equity, stewardship of resources, truth and honesty, compassion and understanding, care for the weak and vulnerable, trust and servanthood are important Christian beliefs, yet are also principles which many others in society sign up to, whatever their own particular worldview.

N T Wright's analogy of Christians engaging in the world today being like writing the fifth act of an unfinished Shakespeare play, is very helpful for Christian governors.[13] Taking into account all that is known about Shakespeare and how he wrote, together with knowledge and understanding of what has gone before in the previous acts of the play, the unfinished script can be acted out. As Christian governors engage within education, we are involved in acting out that fifth act in schools.

In *Supporting Christians in Education,* Trevor Cooling cites the life of Daniel as an example for Christians to follow.[14] Here was a man living with complete integrity, believing in God and practising his religion in a hostile situation, eventually becoming a successful community leader in a secular world. A Christian school governor following Daniel's example will make a valuable contribution, shape for good the outcomes in a school and persuade fellow governors of the rightness of the decision, whilst maintaining the respect of education colleagues and without compromising their Christian faith.

> Nicky was surprised to be described by a wise Christian friend as being eirenic. Having looked it up in the dictionary (it means peacemaking), she realized this was a God-given gift to be developed and practised. She used it to chair governors' meetings, to create a constructive meeting atmosphere, to take the heat out of confrontations and wisely steer opposing groups to negotiated agreement.

Daniel reminds us too that there is no sacred / secular divide in God's economy. We can be called to be a community leader or school governor just as surely as God can call us into ordained ministry. Calvin Seerveld recognized this when, describing his father who was a fishmonger, said, 'My father is in full-time service for the Lord—prophet, priest and king in the fish business.'[15]

The Church's Mission: the Roles of Church and School

In *Churches Linking with Schools,* Howard Worsley outlines ways in which churches can become involved in schools in their parish.[16] There are interesting issues for governors to consider relating to how one contributes to the church's mission. I believe that, whether in a church school or a community school, I am sent out by God to engage with the world and collaborate with the work he is already doing there.[17]

The Lambeth Conference in 1988 adopted the 'Five Marks of Mission.' These were accepted in 1996 by the General Synod, as a summary of what mission is all about.[18] They are:

- To proclaim the good news of the kingdom;
- To teach, baptize and nurture new believers;
- To respond to human need by loving service;
- To seek to transform unjust structures of society;
- To strive to safeguard the integrity of creation and to sustain the life of the earth.

Further discussion about the impact of the Five Marks of Mission in the context of young people and education can be found in *Going for Growth,* published by the Archbishops' Council early in 2010.[19] A useful item on a church school governors' agenda could be to discuss how their church school fulfils the Five Marks of Mission, and should they be considering any new initiatives?

Stephen, the vicar, who was also a foundation governor, realized that many of the children in the village school had not been baptized. Yet he knew that they were old enough to understand what baptism was about. So, as vicar, he discussed baptism during an RE lesson with the Key Stage 2 children. He subsequently wrote a letter to all the parents in which he invited any parents who had not had their children baptized, but who would like to find out more about how to go about this, to contact him. As a consequence of his input to RE lessons, several pupils were very keen to explore this further. Ten families got in touch. Stephen held a series of baptismal classes for the parents, and also for the children who were of school age. The baptism service subsequently included 10% of the school's population and transformed the dynamic of both the village and the school!

In *The Way Ahead: Church of England Schools in the New Millennium,* the missional aspect of being involved in church schools was spelled out.[20] The school and church are close together in partnership: the school and parish church see themselves in active association—as an extended community—together at the heart of the church's mission to the community.

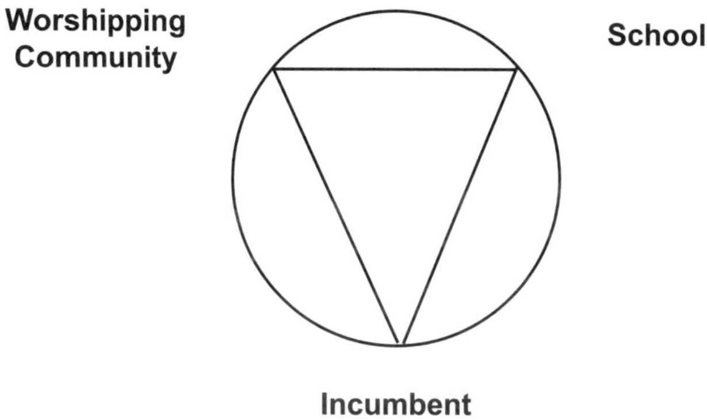

Lydia was an enthusiastic Cub Scout leader. She had been Akala for so many years that she had seen at least two generations of boys pass through. Parents knew her also from the regular parade and family services at church. When she retired from working, she became actively involved in the local church school, voluntarily supporting troubled and troublesome children with activities and lessons. She was delighted to accept when asked to become a community governor. For parents and pupils alike, Lydia made the obvious connection between school and church and they would approach her whenever they needed help or support, or they wanted their children baptizing.

4 The Effective Christian Governor

Responding to God's call to serve as a governor means taking the first steps to making a Christian contribution to the life of a school and its community. It is also the first step on a pathway of continuous learning, not just about education and schools and about strategy, politics, people, economics, budgets and social issues, but also about God's involvement in society, his intentions for humankind, particularly children, and much, much more. I also learned about myself, about using my gifts, talents and skills wisely and about following God's calling in my life.

Training and Learning

The Way Ahead recommended that church school governors should access training wherever possible, and laid an onus on dioceses to provide specific training opportunities. Whatever type of school you serve, governors, as volunteers, have huge responsibilities, so developing governing knowledge and skills is vital. It can be likened to developing a skill or learning a craft, and governors need to be mindful of working towards greater competence. Keeping up to date is important and can be done by reading the useful publications from the National Governors' Association, your Local Authority or diocese, and by accessing a website specifically for Christian governors (see page 26).

Training opportunities are offered by most LAs or dioceses. For clergy and church school governors, diocesan training opportunities usually relate to governors' roles and responsibilities in relation to the distinctive character of church schools. For governors in VA schools, there will be specific training relating to admissions and appeals, to managing buildings and capital projects and to employment of staff.

The Governing 'Body'

Governance is a corporate activity. The fact that governors belong to a governing 'body' reinforces this. But it also provides a useful analogy. In St Paul's references to 'one body, many parts' (1 Corinthians 12.12–30), each member of the body has its own particular function and importance, regardless of how lowly. However, the body is incomplete without any one member and cannot function effectively. This is equally true for a governing body. For good governance, the governors need to function well as a corporate team. Each member of the body may have different roles and functions within the body, but in order for it to work well, the body needs each member to fulfil their part. So, when one member is missing, or there is a vacancy, more pressure is put on the remaining governors and so the governing body is less effective.

> A foundation governor had a very poor attendance record at the governing body. The chairman, also a foundation governor, was concerned about the reputation of the parish church, but also regretted the loss of contribution from the absentee. Meeting together, the chair explained the 'body' analogy, and the colleague governor quickly saw the parallels. He subsequently reprioritized his commitments and made every effort to attend and contribute.

Communicating Effectively

Preparing for a governors' meeting is time well spent, especially when reading briefing papers and reflecting on how best to contribute to the discussion of agenda items. Some governors may need to learn how to communicate their views effectively within the governing body. In a community school, where it may be unwise to assume sympathy and understanding of Christian belief, a Christian governor needs extra skill to communicate effectively, particularly when expressing matters relating specifically to Christian belief.

Jesus communicated his message very effectively whilst on earth, and we have much to learn from his example. He was an active listener and he used lots of clarifying questions (Luke 9.18–20) which were usually open ones beginning with who, what, how, when, where, which and why (Luke 10.36; Luke 18.40).

Just as the incarnation emphasizes the importance of presence and engagement in God's world, we too need to be actively part of the school community. For governors who cannot easily visit school during the working day this can be a challenge, and they need to find other opportunities to get to know the school.

Jesus spoke in the context of powerful action and service; we too can offer practical servant ministry. He used stories to illustrate complex ideas; we can use sharp snapshots to illustrate issues. He argued persuasively but gently when talking to the Samaritan woman at the well (John 4). Like Jesus in that conversation, we would do well to build bridges, offer a better way, explain clearly, suggest appropriate actions, challenge without condemning and make our point clearly.

Christian governors trained by CARE for Education in recent years learned to use the DESC technique to communicate about difficult or controversial issues.[21]

D Describe the facts as clearly and straightforwardly as possible. (Give a brief factual account of the situation.)

E Express your feelings in words. ('As a consequence, I feel concerned / angry / upset…')

S State what you want to see happen. ('I suggest that…')

C Calculate the 'what-ifs.' (Work out in advance what the possible outcomes of the discussion might be and be prepared for each of them.)

Chairing the Governing Body

To be effective, the governors need excellent leadership, so the role of the chair is vital to the outcomes from the governing body. Governors have different gifts and skills; not everyone will make a good chair. St Paul's 'body' analogy should remind a Christian chairperson of the importance of valuing every member's contribution. OFSTED now include, and report on, the effectiveness of the governors in their inspection. Just as knowing your strengths and weaknesses is important for a Christian's personal life, self-assessment of the governing body is good practice. Carrying out a skills audit, or an exercise such as Belbin's team roles with the governing body, helps affirm each member in their own gifting and sometimes helps decide who will make a good chairperson.[22] Having the right person in the chair, together with an effective and knowledgeable clerk, enormously influences the effectiveness of the governors.

Good interpersonal and negotiating skills are essential for a school governor, especially the chairperson. When Tim became vicar and joined the governors, others assumed that he would take up the chairman's position, yet he knew he lacked the necessary skills. It was solved when he subsequently invited a new lay foundation governor to join the governors. It quickly became apparent that the new governor would make a much better chairperson, so the vicar proposed that this person should take over. Having got to know the governing body and evaluated its strengths and weaknesses, the new chairman set about targeting and recruiting others with specific gifts, expertise and skills onto a waiting list to fill vacancies as they occurred.

Equally important is establishing a good relationship between the chair and the head teacher and senior school leaders. This takes time to establish, and will be characterized by trust, respect and honesty. The chair needs to devote time to building this relationship, and to try to be available when needed in an emergency. However, the chair also needs to ensure that the chair/head relationship is never exclusive, making other governors feel as if they just rubber-stamp decisions.

> While she was chair, Ruth occasionally received urgent phone calls to her mobile from the head teacher to seek advice about child protection issues, to report permanent exclusions, early closures due to snow and an overnight break-in and burglary. She also had to make an instant decision to approve the head's decision to close the school with immediate effect when builders discovered asbestos fibres in ceilings on which they were working. To reinforce the corporate nature of governance, Ruth always emailed the rest of the governors with any non-confidential information as soon as she was able.

Meetings between chair and head need to be supportive of the head teacher, yet sufficiently questioning and challenging. Much is written about the fine line between governance and management; a common cause of breakdown in the governor/head relationship happens when governors stray over that line and begin to interfere in the management of the school.

Knowing the School and Succession Planning

When governors make a poor appointment as a head, their decision can stay with the school for many years. The school fails to flourish and the pupils' education suffers. The reputation of the school becomes tarnished, its popularity decreases and the school goes into decline. Appoint a good leader in a school, and the school flourishes. In a church school, appointing a Christian head, or one who will develop the distinctive Christian character of the school, might be an additional challenge.

> As an active parent governor, Bev volunteered in school during the week and knew the school and staff well. After a while, she suggested to the head that she start a prayer group to support the school. Initially unsure, the head subsequently agreed and a group of parents, governors and church members met monthly in the school library to pray. Once staff realized that confidentiality was assured and that people's names were not divulged, they began to add topics for prayer onto the list in the staff room and eventually volunteered answers to prayer and expressed appreciation for the support. The group undertook to support

with prayer the appointment process for a new head. They later joined the www.prayforschools.org network.

Currently, recruitment of senior leaders, particularly head teachers, is an issue for governors in all schools nationally, as there is a huge tranche of school leaders approaching retirement and a shortage of leaders willing to step up to headship. Effective succession planning is important and a key issue for governors today. Knowing your school, particularly the staff, is a vital piece of the jigsaw. If some governors are unable to visit in the school day to get to know staff, it will be important to ensure that some other governors, at least, are able to do this. That enables a head, in discussion with governors, to identify potential leaders and encourage their professional development for leadership.

Governors might have a role to play here in agreeing time out of school for a potential leader to undertake National Professional Qualification for Headship, or to pursue a Church of England School Leadership course. A number of dioceses are currently developing initiatives to develop aspiring leaders for church schools by 'growing their own' from within the diocese, so governors in community schools may also receive requests to support an application from a Christian teacher to pursue such a course.

The issue of encouraging skilled and gifted Christians into the teaching profession, and into school leadership, should be high on churches' agendas. Crucially, it also means that churches need to support Christian teachers once they enter the profession! How to do this is helpfully and constructively explored in *Supporting Christians in Education,* by Trevor Cooling and Mark Greene.

Succession planning within the governing body is equally important. Keeping the membership of the governing body under review, whilst anticipating and planning for replacements whenever possible, is good practice. It is particularly important that foundation governors in church schools are replaced with effective Christian governors in order to maintain the impact of the church in its mission in the school and community.

Called to Serve as a School Governor?

5

When God called him, Moses was at work herding his sheep (Exodus 3 and 4). Moses was fearful that he did not have the gifts, skills or expertise that were needed to do what God wanted of him. Yet God promised that he would go with Moses and equip him with whatever was needed for the given task. When God calls us to serve him, that promise given to Moses remains true for us.

Moses carried a staff; it was the tool of his herdsman's trade, part of his identity, defining who he was. God asked Moses to throw the staff on the ground. As Moses watched, God transformed it! Moses was then commanded to pick up the staff and, in obeying God and doing so, Moses himself was transformed and by God's grace went out to be part of God's mission and enterprise in the world.

God asks the same of his followers today. What do I have in my hand? Not a staff, to be sure. But a modern day equivalent, giving me my identity. As with Moses, God can transform my 'staff' and help me to use it for the benefit of others and to his glory, joining in with what God is doing in my community.[23] God judges our success by our obedience to his call.

God judges our success by our obedience to his call

At the age of 30, long before the Micah challenge became familiar, I sat on the front row of a packed church, as the words spoken at my father's funeral washed around me.[24] Having spent his post-war lifetime working in education, teaching some of Liverpool's most deprived children, my father died suddenly at a relatively young age. 'He has shown you, O man, what is good. And what does the Lord require of you? To act justly and to love mercy and to walk humbly with your God' (Micah 6.8). The vicar chose these words to sum up my father's example and life of service in education. That was when I realized that when we are willing to be and do what God calls us to, then 'We are not merely passing through this world and this life. We are shaping the building blocks of eternity.'[25] This reinforced my calling to serve as a school governor.

6 Resources

Other Relevant Reading

Carol Dadswell, Mike Simmonds with Ann Holt, *Become a Change Activist School Governor* (London: CARE, 2002)

Trevor Cooling with Mark Greene, *Supporting Christians in Education* (London: LICC, 2008)

Other books in the Grove Education Series:

eD 1: Tim Elbourne, *Church Schools: A Mission-shaped Vision*

eD 2: Howard Worsley, *Churches Linking with Schools*

eD 3: Trevor Cooling, *Called to Teach*

Useful Websites

National Governors' Association: www.nga.org.uk

Governors' Ministries, www.transforminggoverning.org.uk

Prayer groups for schools: www.prayforschools.org

Christian teachers: www.transforminglives.org.uk

Notes

1 DCSF, Briefing Information Sheet, *School Governing Bodies—Roles, Responsibilities and Membership*, dated 24/01/06, accessed on www.standards.dfes.gov.uk/.../ School GoverningBodiesBIS.doc?...1 20 December 2009.

2 T Elbourne, *Church Schools: a Mission-shaped Vision* (Grove Education booklet eD1) section 4.

3 J Martin and A Holt, *Joined-up Governance: Making Sense of the Role of the School covernor* (Ely: Adamson Books, 2002) p 112.

4 Archbishops' Council, *The Way Ahead: Church of England Schools in the New Millennium* (London: Church House Publishing, 2001).

5 D Jesson, *Strong Schools for Strong Communities: Reviewing the Impact of Church of England schools in Promoting Community Cohesion* (London: The Church of England Archbishop's Council Education Division, 2009).

6 R Williams, *Christian Distinctiveness in our Academies.* Keynote address at the Church of England Academy Family Launch Conference, Lambeth Palace, 21 October 2009, accessed on 20 December 2009 from www.archbishopofcanterbury.org/2573

7 DCSF, *Securing the Future*, November 2009, encourages collaborative working between schools (for efficiency savings!).

8 R Fung, *The Isaiah Vision* (Geneva: WCC, 1992).

9 The 1988 Education Reform Act required the curriculum to 'promote the spiritual, moral, cultural, mental and physical development of pupils and of society.' The Education (Schools) Act 1992 created the role of Her Majesty's Chief Inspector of Schools, the Office for Standards in Education (OFSTED) and introduced the requirement to inspect 'the spiritual, moral, social and cultural development of pupils.'

10 D Jesson, 2009, *op cit.*

11 This section, 'Seeking the Welfare of the City,' is based on ideas expressed by the Rev'd Dr Richard Cooke in a paper, 'The Church in the City' (12/05/2002) published on Coventry Diocese's website accessed 20 December 2009 from http://www.coventry.anglican.org/ministry/learning/resources/opt/-/item/91

12 P Marshall with L Gilbert, *Heaven is Not My Home: Living in the Now of God's Creation* (Nashville: Word Publishing, 1998) p 58.

13 N T Wright, 'How can the Bible be Authoritative?' *Vox Evangelica*, 1991, 21, 7-32.

14 T Cooling with M Greene, *Supporting Christians in Education* (London: LICC, 2008) p 10.

15 Quoted by P Marshall with L Gilbert, *op cit,* p 72.

16 H Worsley, *Churches Linking with Schools* (Grove Education booklet eD2).

17 T Elbourne, *op cit,* p 8.

18 See http://www.cofe.anglican.org/faith/mission/missionevangelism.html accessed 20 December 2009.

19 Archbishops' Council Education Division, *Going for Growth: Transformation for Children, Young People and the Church* (London 2010) accessed 01/05/2010 from http://www.cofe.anglican.org/info/education/goingforgrowth.pdf

20 *The Way Ahead*, *op cit.*

21 C Dadswell and M Simmonds with A Holt, *Become a Change Activist School Governor* (London: CARE , 2002) p 34.

22 Dr R Meredith Belbin developed a useful analysis of how teams work. See www.belbin.com

23 Based on ideas in a sermon preached by Ken Costa at Holy Trinity Brompton on 22 April 2007.

24 www.micahchallenge.org.uk

25 P Marshall with L Gilbert, *op cit*, p 248.